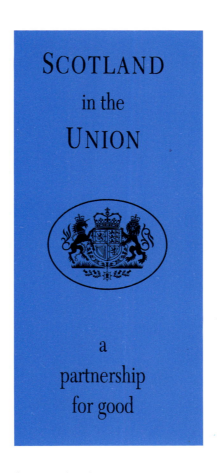

SCOTLAND
in the
UNION

a

partnership
for good

Presented to Parliament by the Secretary of State for Scotland
by Command of Her Majesty
March 1993

Cm 2225   E D I N B U R G H : H M S O   £4.95 net

ISBN 0 10 122252 1

CONTENTS

FOREWORD BY THE PRIME MINISTER

In April 1992 I pledged that the Government would undertake a serious and detailed consideration of Scottish constitutional issues and of Scotland's place in the United Kingdom. To honour that pledge, the Government embarked on a lengthy and wide-ranging examination of the Union of 1707 and the way it works for Scotland. The process became popularly known as "taking stock".

Each of the constituent parts of the United Kingdom has entered into Union with the others by a different route. Each has its own distinctive history, from which the very distinctive qualities of its own community today derive. Great benefits have come to the people of each of its parts from the Union, while the peoples of the United Kingdom have been able to achieve great things largely because they have been together. That is why the Government's commitment to the unity of the Kingdom is so deep.

This White Paper is about the Union with Scotland. That Union is almost 300 years old. As I have said before, no nation could be held irrevocably in a Union against its will and the way it works should be reassessed from time to time, so that it continues to work for the good of all of us. Too often in recent years there has seemed to be in Scotland a genuine, if sometimes unformed, anxiety that the Union is in some way less relevant to Scotland and her aspirations. It is the Government's duty to address that anxiety and that is what this White Paper does.

But this White Paper isn't the end of the story: it is part of an ongoing process. The Union has evolved and changed throughout its history and will continue to do so. Our search for new ways to strengthen the Union will go on. We stand ready to take account of changing circumstances. And our drive to strengthen Scotland's place in the Union - and thus the United Kingdom itself - will continue.

The Act of Union in 1707 was a remarkable political development. The Union it enshrined is an enduring achievement which is to the credit of our people. As we all advance towards its three hundredth anniversary, in 2007, we must reaffirm our faith in the Union and work to ensure that it flowers and flourishes in its fourth century.

March 1993

INTRODUCTION BY THE SECRETARY OF STATE FOR SCOTLAND

The Government's decision to consider ways of improving the government of Scotland and of strengthening Scotland's place in the United Kingdom was prompted by a recognition that there is in Scotland a real concern that the Union may not have been functioning as effectively as it might.

The Government are deeply conscious of the importance of the Union to Scotland and of Scotland to the Union. We believe that the integrity of the Union is critical if Scotland's prominent role within the United Kingdom and the United Kingdom's key role in the outside world are to be maintained.

We believe that in the particular circumstances of Scotland the needs of the Scottish people require that their position within the Union should be strengthened. We believe the proposals for developing the Union which are outlined in this White Paper effectively address such shortcomings as may be perceived in the present arrangements, and that they provide the best reassurance that the needs of the Scottish people will be met.

The Union has yielded, and continues to yield, enormous benefits to Scotland. As part of the United Kingdom, Scotland is able to wield real influence for good around the world, from the United Nations Security Council to the Group of Seven industrial nations the Commonwealth and the European Community. That influence would be lost if Scotland weakened herself within the Union or left the Union altogether.

The maintenance of the Union is essential if Scots are to be able to continue to play our major part in leading the United Kingdom in such a wide variety of fields. In Parliament and in the business community, in the media, trade unions and elsewhere, Scots not only lead Scotland but lead the United Kingdom too. Scotland is thus an outward-looking nation that can be confident of her own position. We form a key part of the leadership of the United Kingdom. With a single act of carelessness, all of that could be lost.

The economic benefits to Scotland of the Union are manifold. Scotland has enjoyed a single market within the Union for 300 years. Resources within the United Kingdom are pooled and distributed by reference to need. The Government recognise Scotland's needs in terms of public expenditure; and are committed to ensuring that those needs are met from general United Kingdom taxation. The maintenance of such a process for allocating resources would be called into serious question if one part of the United Kingdom had unilateral tax-raising powers.

Within the Union special arrangements have evolved to ensure that Scotland's interests are protected and Scotland's identity as a nation enhanced. There are special arrangements for handling Scottish business in Parliament. An entire Department of the Government - The Scottish Office - has responsibility for ensuring that Scotland's priorities and needs are fully taken into account by government as a whole and for ensuring that the Scottish dimension is reflected in the policy of the United Kingdom government. Separate Scottish institutions, for example the legal system and the Universities, have maintained and built on their distinctive Scottish traditions while achieving excellence in the context of the United Kingdom as a whole.

But it is right that, from time to time, all aspects of the way the Union works should be considered and that improvements should be sought. Such a process is essential if the Government are to address the sense of unease which has coloured some Scots' perception of the Union. The Union is good for Scotland, but that does not mean it cannot be made better.

So the Government have sought to identify new ways of building on the existing strengths of the Union, to breathe new life into it. This White Paper should be viewed as a step in that direction.

March 1993

CHAPTER 1
EVOLVING UNION

In considering the future we must understand the past. Within the next 15 years 2 important milestones will be reached in the history of the United Kingdom - in 2003 the 400th anniversary of the Union of the Crowns and in 2007 the 300th anniversary of the Union of the Parliaments. The following paragraphs trace some of the important steps in the evolution of the Union.

1.2   After the Union of the Crowns under James VI of Scotland in 1603 there was no immediate move to unite the countries further and the Scottish Parliament continued to meet in Edinburgh. The Union of the Westminster and Edinburgh Parliaments took place just over a century later in 1707. The Scottish Parliament, having decided that Union was the best way forward for the future relationship with England, passed the Act of Union by a substantial majority. The Westminster Parliament accepted the Act as it stood and the Union was formed. The Act of Union contained 25 Articles providing for the unification of the Kingdoms, the Act of Succession and the creation of one Parliament of Great Britain with a set number of seats for Scottish members. At present Scotland has 72 MPs in the United Kingdom Parliament. If the number of Scottish MPs in the House of Commons reflected Scotland's share of the United Kingdom population that number would be 57. Other Articles provided for a free trade area and economic and fiscal union, and the Treaty as a whole brought Scotland and England together in a full political and economic Union. In this way a framework was established which has proved remarkably fruitful to the present day.

FROM 1707 TO THE PRESENT DAY: THE EXECUTIVE

1.3   Nearly 200 years were to pass from the Act of Union to the establishment of the Office of the Secretary for Scotland in 1885. Until 1745, in continuance of a pre-Union office, a Secretary of State for Scotland was appointed as a member of the Government. During most of the ensuing period formal responsibility for Scottish affairs lay with the Home Secretary advised by the Lord Advocate and by the Scottish Whip. Parliamentary and municipal reforms in the 1830s, which led to more Scottish legislation, kindled interest in establishing a Scottish Minister who would be a political figure. During the following half-century the possibility of restoring the office of Secretary of State was raised on a number of occasions but nothing came of it until the issue was promoted strongly by Lord Rosebery in the early 1880s. He introduced the Secretary for Scotland Bill in 1885, but it fell to Lord Salisbury's Conservative Government of that year to complete the legislation and appoint the Duke of Richmond and Gordon as the first Secretary for Scotland in November 1885. The Office of the Secretary for Scotland was established in Dover House in Whitehall, and this remains the London base of the Secretary of State for Scotland to the present day.

1.4   In its first 40 or so years The Scottish Office comprised a small unit of civil servants providing direct support to the Secretary for Scotland in the exercise of his already wide-ranging responsibilities for Scottish affairs. It was not yet an executive arm of government carrying out functions on behalf of the Minister. For these purposes there existed a number of boards which were based in Edinburgh and which exercised functions in relation to, for example, local government, fisheries, prisons and, later, agriculture.

1.5   A Royal Commission on the Civil Service, which reported just before the outbreak of the First World War, recommended that the Boards be replaced by organisational arrangements similar to those already established in The Scottish Office. This recommendation was not picked up until the late 1920s, by which time Scotland's Minister had been granted the full status of Secretary of State for Scotland. The first holder of this office, Sir John Gilmour, in the Baldwin administration, promoted the Reorganisation of Offices (Scotland) Act 1928 which established the foundations of the modern Scottish Office.

1.6   The next significant development was the transfer of the centre of Scottish administration to Edinburgh. A Committee was set up in 1932 under the chairmanship of Sir John Gilmour (by then no longer Secretary of State for Scotland) to review the Scottish Departments. The Committee recommended that virtually all of the functions then carried out in Dover House should be moved to Edinburgh. A small Edinburgh office had been set up in Edinburgh in 1935 but it was just before the outbreak of the Second World War that St Andrew's House opened for business as the Scottish headquarters of the Secretary of State for Scotland. It consisted of four departments, namely the Department of Agriculture, the Scottish Education Department, the Department of Health and the Scottish Home Department.

1.7   In 1970 the structure of The Scottish Office was strengthened by the creation of a more corporate management system at its centre. It was further strengthened by the establishment of a new Department in the early 1970s in recognition of The Scottish Office's responsibilities in the industrial and economic planning field, responsibilities which were to expand during the later 1970s and 1980s as functions were transferred to The Scottish Office from Whitehall Departments dealing with industry, employment and the environment.

1.8   In Chapter 4 and Annex C the range of functions currently carried out by The Scottish Office on behalf of the Secretary of State is explained and laid out in more detail. That Chapter reveals a steady growth in the range of the Secretary of State's powers from the creation of his office to the present day, and illustrates how the basic framework of the Union has allowed Scottish administration to develop and adapt in response to changing economic and social circumstances while retaining the stability and enduring strength of the Union.

FROM 1707 TO THE PRESENT DAY: THE LEGISLATURE

1.9   The development of the Executive has been parallelled by developments in the legislature. There are significant special arrangements at Westminster for handling Scottish business, where the House of Commons has 3 types of Committee which handle only

Scottish affairs. These are the Scottish Grand Committee, the 2 Scottish Standing Committees and the Select Committee on Scottish Affairs. Also, every 4 weeks during the Parliamentary session, Scottish Office Ministers answer oral Questions in the House of Commons during Scottish Question Time.

1.10   The Scottish Grand Committee, after a brief existence in 1894, was established permanently in 1907. Until recent years its membership included some English MPs as well as all Scottish ones, to reflect the political balance of the House of Commons itself. Its members are now confined to the 72 MPs representing Scottish constituencies. The main functions of the Committee are:

— to debate the general principle of Scottish Bills;

— to debate the Estimates presented to Parliament of Scottish expenditure, normally on not less than 6 days per session (the number can be varied by sessional order); and

— to hold debates, on not more than 6 days per session, on specified matters relating exclusively to Scotland.

1.11   In the 2 Scottish Standing Committees MPs carry out a detailed consideration of Scottish Bills. The Committees function in a similar way to other Standing Committees of the House of Commons. These Committees were introduced in the 1880s to relieve pressure on the House of Commons as a whole. Normally the First Scottish Standing Committee deals with Bills in the Government's main programme, while the Second Standing Committee is mostly concerned with Private Members' Bills.

1.12   The Chairmen of the Scottish Standing Committees, like those of other standing committees, are appointed by the Speaker from the Chairman's panel while the members are nominated by the House of Commons Committee of Selection. For both Chairmen and members this is done on a Bill by Bill basis. In making its nominations the Committee of Selection has to have regard to the balance of parties in the House of Commons as a whole but there must be at least 16 members from Scottish constituencies.

1.13   There is a system of Select Committees which matches the pattern of Government Departments and allows Members of Parliament to question Ministers and officials about the expenditure, administration and policy of their Departments and associated public bodies. Normally once a Select Committee has considered a topic it will publish a report with recommendations. The Government then consider these recommendations and publish a response. As with most other Select Committees of the House of Commons, the membership of the Select Committee on Scottish Affairs reflects the balance of the House.

1.14   Since the Act of Union and in particular over the last 100 years or so there has evolved a framework for the governance of Scotland which is basically sound and which has shown itself adaptable to changing circumstances. Within that framework the increasingly complex tasks of modern government and the requirements of accountability have successfully been accommodated. An important task now is to see what further changes might be made to meet some of the concerns referred to in the introduction and to strengthen the democratic accountability and visibility of government in Scotland.

CHAPTER 2
UNION AND THE SCOTTISH ECONOMY

A SINGLE MARKET SINCE 1707

The union of Scotland with England is one of the oldest economic and monetary unions in the world. From Scotland's viewpoint the union of 1707 was seen as largely an economic matter: it gave Scotland access to markets not only in England but also in the important English territories overseas and ended the earlier, damaging friction between Scotland and England. From England's point of view it gave security within these islands at a time when there was continuing warfare with France.

2.2   The need for free trade with England remains as strong today. England is Scotland's largest market, with over 40 per cent of Scottish manufactured goods being sold within the United Kingdom. Similarly, as part of the United Kingdom today, Scotland has free access to European Community markets and, with the likely extension of the Single Market to include the European Free Trade Association (EFTA) members, except Switzerland, to form the new European Economic Area (EEA) in the very near future, Scottish exporters will have access to an enlarged market which will encompass 18 countries, 378 million consumers, almost 40 per cent of world trade and almost 30 per cent of world production. The European Community is by far Scotland's largest export market and is of growing importance. In 1973 only 23 per cent of Scottish manufactured exports went to the Community. Today that figure is 61 per cent. In all, Scottish manufactured exports to the Community totalled £5.4 billion in 1991 and to the new EEA over £5.9 billion, or two-thirds of total exports. Scotland exports a significantly higher percentage of her manufactured goods to both the European Community and the proposed new EEA than does the United Kingdom as a whole.

2.3   The Single European Market has now been largely completed. The driving force behind the Single Market was the realisation that, if European competitiveness was to be improved and economic growth and social progress maintained, then the abolition of tariffs and quotas between member states was not enough. There were still far too many other factors which continued to restrict trade and these too had to be abolished. Differences in local technical and testing requirements, taxation or purchasing policies which favoured local suppliers, state subsidies and complex trading formalities were some of the obstacles which continued to act as severe barriers to trade even when there were no tariffs at all. But free trade in goods is not a sufficient condition to ensure a genuine free market. There also has to be free movement of people, capital and services. The completion of a genuine

Single Market should reduce business costs and stimulate increased efficiency, and thereby encourage the creation of wealth and jobs. Yet while the people of the European Community have only just managed to achieve a Single Market, Scotland has benefited from such an arrangement for nigh on 300 years. Since 1707 Scotland, as part of the Union, has enjoyed the four freedoms - the freedom of movement of goods, services, people and capital.

2.4   The fact that Scotland is an integral part of these wider areas (the EC and EEA) is undoubtedly an attraction to inward investors in Scotland: such companies set up their manufacturing facilities in Scotland not to serve the Scottish market, nor even simply the UK market, but predominantly the European market and in some cases world markets. The United Kingdom is the world's most popular destination for direct inward investment after the United States of America. Throughout the 1980s the United Kingdom consistently attracted around 40 per cent of all EC inward investment and even in a recession year such as 1991 still managed to attract a third of all EC inward investment, with the next most successful country, France, having less than half the UK share, at 17 per cent.

2.5   Thanks largely to the efforts of Locate in Scotland (LIS) - the Government's inward investment agency - Scotland has secured more than her fair share of the jobs brought by overseas firms locating in the United Kingdom. During the 1980s Scotland secured on average between one fifth and one quarter of all overseas jobs coming to the United Kingdom, which is roughly two and a half times her share of UK employees in employment.

2.6   Since the Second World War the pace of integration of the Scottish economy within the United Kingdom has increased, and developments in the rest of the UK economy have an important effect on Scotland. The level of economic activity can be - and is - influenced by 'supply-side' measures which are designed to improve competitiveness and enhance industrial development - measures such as regional policy, training, research and development and design and marketing policies.

2.7   What has been unique in Scotland is that special institutional arrangements have been developed to deliver these policies. Scottish Enterprise, Highlands and Islands Enterprise - and, before them, the Scottish Development Agency and the Highlands and Islands Development Board - the network of Local Enterprise Companies (LECs), Locate in Scotland, The Scottish Exports Forum and Scottish Trade International have helped to deliver UK economic and industrial policies in an innovative manner, tailored to the needs of the Scottish economy. The Government will continue to lay great stress on refining those institutional arrangements where necessary to ensure that the particular economic needs of Scotland are met within the framework of UK economic policy.

PUBLIC EXPENDITURE AND REVENUE IN SCOTLAND

2.8   The balance of expenditure and revenue in Scotland is a key issue in assessing the economic benefits of the Union.

2.9   The Scottish Office published in March 1992 a document "Government Expenditures and Revenues in Scotland" which brought together all the available facts and figures about Government expenditure and revenue in Scotland. It examined the complete range of government spending in Scotland – those programmes which are the direct responsibility of the Secretary of State, programmes of other Government Departments which have an identifiable impact on Scotland and Scotland's share of public expenditure which is incurred on behalf of the United Kingdom as a whole.

2.10   The publication showed that in 1990-91 (the latest year for which all the figures are available) total public expenditure per head in Scotland was estimated to be just over 12 per cent higher than in the United Kingdom as a whole.

2.11   Revenue raised in Scotland from income tax, National Insurance contributions, Value Added Tax and local authority revenue – which together account for about two-thirds of total tax revenue raised in Scotland – is lower than the UK average per head. It seems likely that total aggregate revenues are also slightly lower.

2.12   Under the present constitutional arrangements, therefore, Scotland derives substantial economic and financial benefit from the Union.

2.13   The Secretary of State for Scotland's spending programmes fall into two main categories; those within the Scottish block and those outside it. The programmes outside the block are mainly those where there is a requirement for a standard policy across Great Britain or the United Kingdom. Planned spending outside the block is settled by separate negotiation.

2.14   For the programmes within the block a different procedure applies. Under the rules which apply to territorial Departments, Scotland (like Wales and Northern Ireland) automatically takes a proportion of changes to expenditure plans in the annual public expenditure survey for comparable expenditure by non-territorial or Whitehall Departments. That proportion is calculated by reference to a population-related formula which was updated in the 1992 Public Expenditure Survey, to take account of the results of the 1991 census, so that it is now 10.66 per cent of spending changes in England. The Secretary of State's block programmes emerged from the 1992 Survey with spending in Scotland over 30 per cent higher on a per capita basis than spending on comparable services in England.

2.15   It has been the Government's policy that the Secretary of State's programme of public expenditure should not be reduced below Scotland's fair share based on her relative needs. The Government will continue with this approach.

2.16   The Secretary of State for Scotland is able to allocate the resources within his block (95 per cent of the total resources available to him in the 1992 Survey) according to his perception of the needs and priorities of Scotland. The Government believe this discretion is vital to ensuring that public spending yields the maximum benefit in Scotland.

CONCLUSION

2.17   The Union in 1707 increased dramatically the size of Scotland's domestic economy and made her part of a larger, more powerful economy. Scotland, as part of the United Kingdom, is a member of the G7 - the most industrialised and economically powerful countries in the world. And as a participant in the Single European Market, Scotland is part of the strongest economic block in the world.

2.18   Scotland continues to derive enormous economic, trade and investment benefits from being part of the United Kingdom and, in turn, part of the wider European Community. In addition Scotland contributes less than her population share to the UK Exchequer, while receiving more than her population share from public expenditure programmes. For three centuries the Union has been the cornerstone of Scotland's prosperity and it remains crucial to Scotland's economic success.

CHAPTER 3
SCOTLAND'S LEGAL SYSTEM

As the introduction indicated, one of the most important features of the Treaty of Union was its provision for securing the independence of the Scottish legal system. Article XIX of the Treaty expressly guarantees the independence of the supreme Scots civil and criminal courts, while Article XVIII provides that no changes should be made "in laws which concern private right, except for evident utility of the subjects within Scotland". The Treaty thus expressly safeguarded the two main elements of the Scottish system, namely, the court structure through which justice is administered and the body of rules and principles by which justice is determined.

3.2   The Court of Session and the High Court of Justiciary function entirely independently of the Supreme Court of Judicature for England and Wales. The High Court of Justiciary continues to be the final court of appeal in criminal cases. Although the House of Lords has succeeded to the appellate jurisdiction of the Scots Parliament in civil cases, it exercises this jurisdiction through its judicial committee, at least two members of which are always highly respected Scots lawyers who have usually served as judges in the Court of Session.

3.3   The independence of the Scottish legal system is also reflected in the appointment of Law Officers for Scotland, the Lord Advocate and the Solicitor General for Scotland. The Lord Advocate is the head of the independent public prosecution service. The Scottish Law Officers advise the Government on legal matters affecting Scotland and share with the Government's other Law Officers the duty of advising on European Community law as it affects the United Kingdom. The Scottish Law Officers may represent the United Kingdom before the European Court and other international bodies, particularly when an issue of Scottish interest is concerned. The Lord Advocate also gives advice on the appointment of Scottish judges. In addition he is a member of two Cabinet Committees and may attend meetings of others where the business makes this desirable.

3.4   The nature of the Scottish Law Officers' role makes it desirable that at least one of them should be in Parliament. This has been achieved in practice by the convention that has evolved in recent years that, if he is not a member of either House, the Lord Advocate is made a member of the House of Lords.

THE MUTUAL BENEFITS OF UNION

3.5   The existence of separate legal systems is a good example of the mutual benefits of the Union. Each system enjoys the benefits of close association but in a way which ensures that each retains its independent identity and preserves its traditional strengths.

3.6   Scots law has been particularly successful since the inception of the Union in preserving its existing rules and concepts where they continue to work well. When drafting new legislation great care is now taken to try to ensure that valued elements of existing Scots legal concepts are not prejudiced. There is little doubt that this resilience has been of great benefit to Scotland. In the area of criminal law, for example, whose foundation is still the body of general principles formulated by the institutional writers of the 19th century, Scots law has shown itself highly adaptable.

3.7   The existence of separate legal systems has also however brought wider benefits. The fact of the Union and the greater degree of co-operation which it necessitated assisted greatly in the development of each system. Comparative experience has proved an important source of the motivation and ideas for reform. One consequence of the remarkable circumstance of having different legal systems within one state is to increase the likelihood of such comparative experience being gained. This leads to benefits arising both from cross fertilisation and from the creative tension of legal debate among practitioners of the individual systems.

3.8   This close association has led to co-operation in effective law enforcement, stemming from the mutual respect and shared values of the Courts throughout the United Kingdom. This has always been important in the fight against crime. It is of particular benefit when much crime is no longer only local. For instance, there is simpler enforcement of warrants in the United Kingdom than elsewhere in Europe. Standing arrangements between the Home Office, Scottish Office and the Crown Office will be maintained to resolve any technical obstacles which arise.

3.9   Equally the arrangements are flexible enough to ensure that in areas of law in which uniformity is desirable (for example commercial law and consumer protection law) necessary provisions are now embodied in legislation applying in the same essential terms throughout the United Kingdom.

A MODERN LEGAL SYSTEM

3.10   The principal purpose of a legal system must be to provide effective and efficient administration of justice for those over whom it has jurisdiction. Clearly, that purpose can be achieved only if the legal system can adapt and develop in keeping with changing social circumstances. Despite the innate adaptability of the Scottish system the pace of change in social circumstances makes it necessary to keep the law up-to-date, particularly in the commercial field. The Scottish legal system has to be given every assistance in meeting the challenge which this represents. This suggests the need to look critically at current Parliamentary procedures to see whether ways can be found to expedite them and thus to facilitate essential law reform. Chapter 6 describes the outcome of the Government's examination of this matter.

CHAPTER 4
SCOTLAND'S DEPARTMENT IN GOVERNMENT

Fundamental to an appreciation of the way in which Scottish affairs are handled within the Union in the last decade of the 20th century is an understanding of the role of the Secretary of State for Scotland and of The Scottish Office. The Scottish Office is Scotland's Department in the Government but in general the Scottish people have never been been as aware as they might be of the influence of the Secretary of State and his Office within the United Kingdom Government, how that is to Scotland's benefit and of the extent to which it means decision-making is devolved to Scotland.

SCOTLAND'S VOICE AT THE CENTRE OF GOVERNMENT: POLICY FORMATION AND DELIVERY.

4.2   Nowadays the Secretary of State has responsibility as Cabinet Minister for a wide range of statutory functions in Scotland which in England and Wales are the responsibility of a number of departmental Cabinet Ministers. He is assisted by a team of Ministers: the current allocation of responsibilities among the Minister of State and the Parliamentary Under Secretaries of State is shown in Annex A. He also works closely with Ministers in charge of other Departments on topics of significance to Scotland within their fields of responsibility. The Secretary of State's close involvement with other Cabinet colleagues in key-decision making at the centre is demonstrated in his membership of a number of standing Ministerial Committees, Sub-committees and Working Groups. (These are listed in Annex B.) Scotland thus plays her full part in shaping policy for the United Kingdom as a whole. In promoting improvements to the governance of Scotland, the Government are determined to keep Scotland's strong voice at the heart of the government of the United Kingdom.

4.3   The Secretary of State's responsibilities include education, health, social work, law and order, agriculture and fisheries, environmental protection and conservation of the countryside, land-use planning, local government, housing, roads and certain aspects of transport services. He is the lead Minister for forestry in Great Britain.

4.4   The Secretary of State also has a major role in relation to the Scottish economy and in particular has important functions relating to industrial development, with responsibility for financial assistance to industry. He is responsible for the strategic direction and funding of non-departmental public bodies such as Scottish Enterprise, Highlands and

Islands Enterprise, New Town development corporations and the Scottish Tourist Board. (More information about non-departmental public bodies is contained in Annex C.) The Secretary of State plays a full part in determining energy policy, particularly in relation to the electricity supply industry in Scotland. He takes responsibility for government involvement in a range of other functions from fire services to sport. Finally, the Secretary of State has supervisory responsibility for legal services in Scotland and is advised by the Scottish Law Officers, the Lord Advocate and the Solicitor General for Scotland.

4.5   All of this illustrates the extent to which the Secretary of State and his Ministers are able to tailor Government policy to meet the distinctive needs of Scotland. The Secretary of State is able both to initiate policy in accordance with Scotland's own priorities (and often export that policy to other parts of the United Kingdom) and also refine UK-wide policy to take account of particular Scottish circumstances. The Government are keen to encourage a distinctively Scottish approach to policy-making where that is in the interests of Scotland and renewed emphasis will be placed on identifying Scottish solutions for Scottish problems.

4.6   In discharging their responsibilities the Secretary of State and his Ministers are assisted by the civil servants in The Scottish Office. This involves some 13,413 staff employed in The Scottish Office and Associated Departments, of whom 4,577 are in the Scottish Prison Service. (More details are given in Annex D.) While the majority of staff in The Scottish Office are based in the central belt, other staff work from offices around the country including Dumfries, Oban, Inverness and Thurso. A number also work in the Scottish Office's London base, Dover House in Whitehall. The Government will support and encourage more secondments between The Scottish Office and Whitehall Departments.

THE SCOTTISH OFFICE: AIMS AND OBJECTIVES

4.7   The main aim of The Scottish Office is to create an environment in which the public and private sectors work together to improve the economic, social and environmental conditions in which people in Scotland live and work.

4.8   The main general objectives of The Scottish Office are as follows:

> — to encourage Scottish industry directly or through sponsored bodies and in particular competitive firms, entrepreneurship, inward investment, exporting and training;
>
> — to secure improvements in the health of the people of Scotland and in the operation of their health service;
>
> — to seek improvements in the quality of provision of Scottish education at all levels;
>
> — to promote agriculture and fisheries in Scotland;
>
> — to assist in the improvement of the quality of housing in Scotland;
>
> — to promote environmental protection and nature conservation in Scotland;

— to provide a framework for effective and accountable local government;

— to secure an efficient roads and transport network; and

— to support the Scottish police, fire and prison services.

4.9   The specific functions, aims and objectives of each part of The Scottish Office are kept under review to ensure that they are relevant and that they reflect developments and changes in policies. While the broad objectives for each department tend to be constant, the key challenges change from year to year as objectives are achieved.

4.10   In short, the Office of the Secretary of State for Scotland and its associated strong supporting administrative and financial arrangements provide Scotland with an effective and integrated system of executive Government. Government alone cannot solve Scotland's problems - no Government can - but a well established and adaptable framework exists within which policies can be pursued that reflect Scotland's needs and appropriate action can be taken, whether within the United Kingdom or within the European Community. This situation is not always well understood. Chapters 7 to 9 consider how the existing arrangements might be further developed.

CHAPTER 5
SCOTLAND IN EUROPE

The affairs of the European Community are playing an increasingly important part in Scottish life. The Secretary of State's membership of the Government of one of the most influential EC Member States ensures Scotland a strong voice in formulating Community policy. The Scottish Office participates fully in the UK governmental machinery which determines the UK negotiating stance in EC discussions and is represented in Brussels by the Office of the UK Permanent Representative (UKREP) which is able to bring the whole weight of UK influence to bear in pursuing within the Community policies in which Scottish interests have been fully taken into account.

5.2   Scottish Ministers and Scottish Office officials can and do contribute at relevant meetings of the Council of Ministers and of the Working Groups which prepare Council business across the policy spectrum. It is very much in Scotland's interest that these arrangements should continue.

5.3   Most critical decisions affecting the future of the European Community are taken at meetings of the Council of Ministers. The present arrangements mean that Scottish interests are represented by a large and powerful member of the European Community. In order to gain full advantage of these arrangements for Scotland, Scottish Ministers and Scottish Office officials will take part in an increasing number of meetings of the Council of Ministers. By having direct access to the Council of Ministers, Scotland is strongly represented in Europe.

SCOTLAND'S PROFILE IN EUROPE

5.4   Scotland is also, of course, represented in other institutions of the European Community through Members of the European Parliament and of the Economic and Social Committee. Ratification of the Maastricht Treaty will bring with it the establishment of the Committee of the Regions, providing a new forum for the expression of Scottish opinion. This new Committee will give Scotland an additional voice at the centre of Community affairs and it will complement the work of the other Community institutions. The Committee will also be an effective channel for the expression of the legitimate interests of the nations and regions of Europe. In determining membership of the Committee, the Government will ensure that Scotland has substantial representation on it.

5.5   These arrangements will not in any way exclude the full use of other, less formal mechanisms. In 1992 the Government approved the establishment of Scotland Europa by Scottish Enterprise, to act in Brussels on behalf of a wide range of Scottish private and public sector organisations. This important initiative will be of considerable assistance to Scottish businesses seeking to break into European markets and will also enable key Scottish organisations to have early and accurate information about developments in the Community. In addition it will help them to establish contacts with the Commission and other member states. It will effectively complement the work of UKREP.

5.6   As a great trading nation, Scotland is poised to benefit enormously from the European Single Market. In order to help Scottish exporters take advantage of the opportunities of the Single Market, the Secretary of State established in 1991 Scottish Trade International, an agency comprising Scottish Office and Scottish Enterprise staff. The central priority for this agency must be to help Scottish exporters capitalise on the challenges of the Single Market. To ensure that this priority is achieved, the Government will review the operation of Scottish Trade International.

5.7   The Government are determined to ensure that Scotland enjoys as high a profile as possible in Europe. It is important that Scotland should establish her own links with other parts of Europe with which she has many interests in common. That is why, for example, the Government have taken significant steps to foster links between Scotland and Bavaria. The Government will continue to foster such European links. They are also keen to encourage other organisations to assist in achieving this goal. Local authorities have been active in establishing their own networks with other European regions, cities and municipalities, a process which the Government support and will continue to encourage. The Government also welcome the innovative approach of Scottish Financial Enterprise in taking the lead in establishing in 1992 the Association of European Regional Financial Centres. Initiatives of this kind will be supported and encouraged by the Government in order to help Scotland make the most of the many opportunities that Europe offers.

EUROPARTENARIAT

5.8   A Europartenariat is a major event which offers an outstanding opportunity for hundreds of companies across the European Community to come together in one place to meet potential business partners. Funded by the European Commission and the host country, from both public and private sectors, the Europartenariat is a tremendous stimulus for cross-Europe trade and business. In recognition of this, and of the importance of maintaining Scotland's profile in Europe, the Government will, in cooperation with the EC Commission, host a Europartenariat in Glasgow in December 1993. Following the success of the European Council in Edinburgh, the Europartenariat event will be a major boost to the Scottish economy and is a further illustration of Scotland's important place in Europe.

CONCLUSION

5.9   The European Community is involved in almost every aspect of Scottish life. It is vital that Scotland's voice should be heard in Europe and under the existing arrangements Scotland is strongly represented in Brussels. The Government have taken steps to complement and add to that strong representation to ensure that there is a multi-pronged approach to promoting Scotland's interests in Europe. As Europe continues to develop, the Government will keep under review Scotland's profile in Europe to ensure it matches Scottish needs.

CHAPTER 6
THE WAY AHEAD: SCOTLAND IN PARLIAMENT

The earlier chapters of the White Paper have shown how, within the Union, arrangements for the governance of Scotland have been able to develop in a flexible and pragmatic way. That should be a continuing process and it is important that the arrangements are kept under regular review. The Government will certainly continue to do so and this White Paper is not intended to represent the last word on the subject. The review which has taken place since the last Election has suggested that a number of further developments would be appropriate at this time. These are designed to improve the efficiency and effectiveness with which the public affairs of Scotland are handled. They concern both the machinery of Parliament and of the Government. This Chapter deals with Parliamentary procedures, Chapter 7 discusses Government machinery, Chapter 8 outlines proposals to create a more responsive Scottish Office and Chapter 9 discusses plans for the diffusion of power within Scotland.

PARLIAMENTARY PROCEDURES

6.2   A frequent criticism of Scotland's place in the Union has been that Westminster is remote; that there is insufficient time in its crowded schedule for Scottish affairs to be fully and properly discussed; and in particular that the opportunities it provides to hold Scottish Office Ministers accountable for policy in Scotland are inadequate, given the range of Scottish Office responsibilities. It is often argued that there should be more scope for Scottish legislation to keep up with developments south of the Border, to implement measures of Scottish Law Reform more promptly and to provide greater opportunities to make changes, unique to Scotland, which require legislation.

6.3   It is also suggested from time to time that there are few opportunities for general debate on subjects where there is a unique or predominant Scottish interest, and that even in debates on UK-wide matters the (sometimes different) Scottish dimension receives insufficient attention.

6.4   Some of these criticisms have merit but in the Government's view they do not represent an entirely fair picture. The need for a solid programme of Scottish legislation is, and has been for many years, an accepted part of the planning of the legislative programme in Parliament. In the past decade around 60 Scottish Bills have been enacted. In addition, great care is taken to ensure that, where amendments to Scottish statutes are contained in GB or UK Bills, those are prepared by the Scottish Parliamentary draftsmen in a way which preserves the integrity of the Scottish statute book, and that there is ample opportunity for the Scottish provisions to be debated. And, of course, Scottish MPs are able to contribute

SCOTLAND IN THE UNION
A PARTNERSHIP FOR GOOD

fully to Parliamentary consideration of matters not just of particular interest to Scotland but also concerning the United Kingdom as a whole.

6.5   In recent years changes to Westminster procedures have been made which provide a greater opportunity for the consideration of Scottish matters. In 1979 the system of Select Committees relating to Government Departments was established, and the Select Committee on Scottish Affairs has been an important and valuable mechanism in the Parliamentary scrutiny of Government business in Scotland including fieldwork and meetings in Scotland as well as at Westminster. Following a period between 1987 and 1992 when agreement could not be reached on the constitution of the Committee, the Government are glad that its re-establishment has now been achieved and look forward to the further development of its work.

6.6   Recent years have also seen a development in the role of the Scottish Grand Committee, which comprises all the Members of Parliament representing constituencies in Scotland. In the 1981-82 Session provision was introduced for the Committee to meet from time to time on Mondays in Edinburgh and the first meeting took place on 15 February 1982. The Committee has held a wide range of debates each year since, both in Edinburgh and at Westminster, and has also taken the Second Reading debates of some Scottish legislation.

PLANNED DEVELOPMENTS

6.7   While, within the Union, the ultimate authority of Parliament at Westminster must remain paramount, the Government accept that there is scope for further improvements in the way in which Scottish matters are handled. The objective is to find ways of handling Commons business relating to Scotland, including legislation, which maximise the involvement of Members of Parliament for Scottish constituencies and increase the responsiveness of the system to Scottish considerations without impeding the crucial ability of Scottish MPs to play their full part in considering in Parliament issues affecting the whole of the United Kingdom. The following proposals are designed to build on and improve the existing Parliamentary mechanisms for handling Scottish business, covering legislation (both primary and secondary) and providing added opportunities for thorough debate and discussion of matters of particular concern in Scotland.

6.8   The main proposals offer a systematic and progressive widening of the range of business to be handled by the Scottish Grand Committee, meeting when appropriate in Scotland as well as at Westminster. They also offer the possibility of improved scrutiny of Scottish legislation through the use of provisions for Special Standing Committees to meet, in Scotland if appropriate, to take evidence on Scottish Bills. At the heart of these proposals is a desire to make government in Scotland more accountable without weakening Scotland's special position at the Parliament of the Union. The objective of increasing the scrutiny by Parliament of the Secretary of State for Scotland, his Ministers and his Departments is desirable in itself and is especially important given the expansion of his responsibilities in recent years.

SCOTTISH GRAND COMMITTEE

6.9   The following paragraphs set an agenda for the development of the role of the

24

Scottish Grand Committee both in handling legislation and in providing increased opportunities for general debate and discussion of Scottish matters.

LEGISLATION

6.10   The consideration of the principle of a Bill - its Second Reading - normally involves a debate on the floor of the House of Commons. The Bill is then committed to a Standing Committee for line by line consideration. In the case of Scottish Bills provision already exists to appoint a Scottish Standing Committee, which must contain at least 16 Members representing Scottish constituencies. There is also provision for a Second Scottish Standing Committee, and this is generally appointed when required to consider Private Members' Bills relating exclusively to Scotland. The Bill is then returned to the floor of the House of Commons for its Report Stage, normally involving a debate at which further amendments may be considered. The last stage is the Third Reading, which gives the House of Commons a final opportunity to consider and, if it so decides, approve the Bill in its finally amended form.

6.11   Provision has existed in Standing Orders since 1948 for the consideration of the principle of Bills relating exclusively to Scotland to be debated in the Scottish Grand Committee. This is intended to dispense with the need for a Second Reading debate on the floor of the House. When the Scottish Grand Committee has considered the principle of the Bill, Second Reading can be moved formally in the House and, if necessary, put to a vote without debate.

6.12   So far relatively little use has been made of this procedure but the Government believe that it is capable of development, given goodwill on all sides. This would enable a wider range of Bills to be handled in the uniquely Scottish forum of the Scottish Grand Committee, enabling more account to be taken of Scottish opinion during their consideration in principle, thus allowing a fuller Scottish legislative programme. For this approach to succeed all sides will have to agree that the Scottish Grand Committee debate is the substantive consideration of the principle of the Bill: delaying or disruptive tactics would undermine the approach and rob it of its value. The need for formal approval of Second Reading by the whole House would of course remain and could involve a vote if necessary.

6.13   There are three possible categories of Bill to which the approach could gradually be extended:-

Government Bills

The Government's legislative programme, announced in the Queen's Speech, normally contains a number of significant Scottish measures. There could be distinct advantages in bringing before the Committee a wider range of programme measures than has hitherto been the case, if it was agreed that they could be handled in the way discussed above. This would not of course undermine the continuing entitlement of Scottish Bills to have their Second Reading debates, if preferred, on the floor of the House.

Law Reform Bills

The Scottish Law Commission is responsible for a programme of review of the law of Scotland and its work generally leads to proposals for law reform, often in the shape of draft

Bills on which consultation is conducted. In their response to the recent report of the Jellicoe Committee on the Committee Work of the House of Lords, the Government have acknowledged that it would be desirable to find ways of significantly increasing the through-put of Law Reform Bills proposed by the Law Commissions if this can be done without prejudice to the main programme set out in the Queen's Speech. Increased use of the Scottish Grand Committee to consider the principle of Scottish Law Reform Bills would contribute to this objective.

Private Members' Bills

Where a Private Member's Bill relates exclusively to Scotland it may be appropriate to take the opportunity of debating its principle in the Scottish Grand Committee, though it would be necessary to ensure that the Bill's remaining stages continued to be subject to the timetabling and other requirements which applied to Private Members' Bills generally. Thus the value of this approach would lie in an opportunity for proper debate of the issues rather than in accelerating the progress of such Bills.

6.14   Similar considerations apply to subordinate legislation, by means of which provision is made for rules and regulations, grant schemes and other detailed matters required to implement primary legislation. In general, subordinate legislation of major importance requires to be approved by Parliament in draft before coming into effect ("Affirmative Resolutions"). Less important matters do not require positive approval before they take effect, but if they are opposed a debate may be held ("Negative Resolutions"). Subordinate legislation thus can often provide an opportunity to debate matters of considerable practical and political importance, such as the annual Revenue Support Grant, Housing Support Grant and Legal Aid orders and the orders which often form part of the implementation process of primary legislation; handling these in a uniquely Scottish forum offers important advantages. The Government propose a new procedure allowing for the debates on Affirmative Resolutions and on prayers against Negative Resolutions to be referred to the Scottish Grand Committee. Such debates would be on consideration in principle. As with Bills, an understanding would be required that the consideration in principle would be agreed, and the matter would require approval by the House of Commons itself, involving a vote if necessary.

DELIBERATIVE DEBATES

6.15   At present the Scottish Grand Committee may have up to 6 general debates each session on "matter days" and must have at least 6 debates on "estimates days" if Estimates for which the Secretary of State is responsible are referred to it. The full entitlement has tended not to be taken in recent years and the timing of the publication of the Estimates has led to the bunching of those debates in the summer. The Government propose to abandon the distinction between "matter days" and "estimates days", providing instead for up to 12 general debates, and to make explicit provision that the subject for a specified number of these should be chosen by the opposition parties in Scotland. Used flexibly, these arrangements will provide a valuable new opportunity for constructive and regular debate of current issues. One subject which is likely to be appropriate for debate in this way is the allocation each year by the Secretary of State of the public expenditure resources at his disposal. The Committee could also be given the opportunity to debate the reports published by the Scottish Affairs Select Committee of the House of Commons. As at present, double debates could sometimes take place, by agreement, lasting 5 hours instead of 2½. Also, as at present, the Committee could sometimes meet in Edinburgh - and perhaps elsewhere in Scotland. Such arrangements would be without prejudice to the continuing rights of Government and opposition parties to debate Scottish matters, as at present, on the floor of the House of Commons.

QUESTION TIME

6.16   The present Questions rota of the House of Commons provides for Oral Questions to Scottish Office Ministers once every 4 weeks. The Government believe that the extensive range of business for which the Secretary of State for Scotland is now responsible, equivalent as it is to that of several Whitehall Departments, provides justification for augmenting this by providing an additional Question Time at certain meetings of the Scottish Grand Committee. This could be modelled on existing practice, a specified time at the beginning of certain Sittings being set aside for Questions to Scottish Office Ministers, tabled in advance, and with the opportunity for cross-examination through Supplementaries. Alternatively the Government are willing to consider modifying the present format on these occasions. For example, a more flexible approach, perhaps akin to the Starred and Unstarred Question procedures already used in the House of Lords, would allow more detailed consideration of a smaller number of questions. This is an area which the Government would be willing to explore with other parties.

6.17   The Scottish Office Minister in the House of Lords is usually responsible for a substantial range of departmental functions, accounting for a large proportion of the resources at the disposal of the Scottish Office. At present, Scottish Members of Parliament have only very limited opportunities to examine the Minister in question, in the context of examination by the Select Committee on Scottish Affairs of particular topics. The Select Committee comprises only 11 members. The Government believe that it would strengthen the arrangements for publicly examining the policies and work of the Scottish Office if a means could be found of enabling its House of Lords Minister - and also the Lord Advocate, Scotland's senior Law Officer, who is at present a Member of the House of Lords - to give evidence to the Scottish Grand Committee. The Government therefore envisage a new procedure, analogous to Select Committee procedure but unique to the Scottish Grand Committee. Subject to consultation and agreement between both Houses, the format envisaged is that the Minister, with his agreement, would be permitted to make a brief statement on a particular topic specified in advance and would then be questioned on the subject for a set period. In this way, Scottish Members of Parliament would be able to examine in depth the Scottish Office Minister in the House of Lords and the Lord Advocate about their responsibilities. The proposed procedure would also apply to other Scottish Office Ministers, enabling them to be examined in depth when appropriate.

STATEMENTS

6.18   A possible additional development would be to make provision for Oral Statements to be made by Scottish Office Ministers in the course of Scottish Grand Committee Sittings.

In practice, the need to make announcements to Parliament often arises at short notice and it would be impossible to have hard and fast rules about when a Statement to the Scottish Grand Committee would be appropriate. In the Government's view, however, it is sensible to make provision for this so that it can be done when it is suitable. At the same time they recognise that the right of all United Kingdom Members of Parliament to hear and question Oral Statements should not be unduly constrained.

ADJOURNMENT DEBATES

6.19   Finally, the Government propose that provision should be made for short Adjournment debates, on the Westminster model, at the end of Sittings of the Scottish Grand Committee. It is acknowledged in Westminster that these provide a valuable opportunity at the end of each day's business on the floor of the House for Members to raise at relatively short notice issues of particular concern, often of a constituency nature. It seems valuable to extend the opportunity to the Scottish Grand Committee. As in Westminster, there would be a ballot some days before the meeting of the Scottish Grand Committee and a limited period, no more than 30 minutes, would be provided for the debate including the Minister's response. The subject matter would be confined to the responsibilities of Scottish Office Ministers. Again, the rights of Members for Scottish constituencies to seek Adjournment debates on the floor of the House of Commons would remain unaffected.

PROCEDURE FOR IMPLEMENTATION

6.20   Some of these changes would require amendments to Standing Orders and the Government will bring these forward for discussion in due course. The new framework will in effect provide an agenda for the development of the role of the Scottish Grand Committee in ways which increase its involvement in, and relevance to, Scottish affairs. At each stage the Government will be testing the success and acceptability of the changes and will wish to see evidence that they are being used constructively before building on them. It is not therefore possible to quantify at this stage the amount of additional business which will be handled by the Scottish Grand Committee. The basic schedule of general debates might occupy up to 12 Sittings, at fairly regular intervals, whether at Westminster or in Scotland. The Question Time could be scheduled for every second or third Sitting, on a basis which avoided too close a coincidence with the House of Commons rota for Scottish Office Questions. The Government see attractions in holding the majority of these Sittings in Edinburgh or other parts of Scotland and they are willing to discuss these proposals with other parties and to consider varying the format as matters proceed.

6.21   Overall, this approach offers the prospect of a significant increase in the opportunities for Parliamentary business of particular concern to Scotland to be handled in a uniquely Scottish forum, reducing the remoteness for which Westminster is criticised and, with co-operation on all sides, providing increased opportunities for Scottish legislation to reach the Statute Book.

SPECIAL STANDING COMMITTEE

6.22   The Standing Orders of the House of Commons contain provision for Bills to be referred after Second Reading to a Special Standing Committee as an alternative to an ordinary Standing Committee. The Special Standing Committee may meet on up to 4 occasions over a period of 28 days taking oral evidence about the Bill. The record of that evidence, and written evidence which the Committee may order to be printed, is available as background to inform the Committee's subsequent line by line consideration of the Bill, which proceeds as in an ordinary Standing Committee. This provision has been little used - and never for Scottish legislation - being considered in general to be appropriate only for relatively non-controversial measures with a degree of cross-party support, where technical evidence from specialists or interest groups would have a particularly important part to play in the detailed consideration of the Bill's provisions.

6.23   In the Government's view the mechanism does, however, provide a particularly appropriate response to certain uniquely Scottish circumstances. There is a separate body of Scots law administered through a separate legal system. In many areas which are subject to legislation there exist in Scotland separate professional or other expert bodies with unique experience and an individual contribution to offer. They may feel remote from the Westminster process and may not have the same opportunity as their comparators south of the Border to influence the consideration of legislation during its passage at Westminster. The Special Standing Committee procedure provides an opportunity to remedy this by establishing a mechanism for evidence to be taken, possibly in Scotland, before line by line consideration of a Bill begins.

6.24   Proposals for detailed changes to the relevant Standing Orders will be brought forward in due course. The Government envisage that these will involve a development of the existing provisions for Special Standing Committees in a number of ways to suit Scottish circumstances. The Committee would meet to agree its method of working and the range of interests from which it wished to take evidence, and would have power to hold its oral evidence-taking sessions in Scotland if it wished. Its further meetings, in Westminster, would handle the line by line examination of the Bill in the normal way. In order not to delay the consideration of legislation it would remain subject to the 28 day time limit for evidence-taking which at present applies to Special Standing Committees.

CONCLUSION

6.25   The Government believe that, taken together, these proposals provide a basis for a substantial and worthwhile improvement in the handling of Parliamentary business relating to Scotland. They emphasise the important role of all Scottish Members of Parliament. They also provide a basis for making Scottish Ministers more accountable. They are an agenda for progressive change, over a period of time, to be introduced flexibly in the light of experience. Clearly, their successful introduction and operation will depend on goodwill from politicians in Scotland. The Government offer them as a constructive response to the aspirations of the people of Scotland to see a Parliamentary process which is less remote and takes more account of their interests and concerns, and are confident that they can make an important contribution to meeting those aspirations.

CHAPTER 7
THE WAY AHEAD:
GOVERNMENT IN SCOTLAND

Chapter 4 and the Annexes to it describe in some detail the current central government arrangements based on the role of the Secretary of State. The process of progressive administrative devolution of powers and functions to the Secretary of State has greatly expanded his role in recent years in fields as diverse as economic development and training and nature conservation. Further administrative devolution of this kind will take effect in April when the Secretary of State assumes responsibility for higher education in Scotland.

7.2   The extension of administrative devolution is very much in line with the Government's desire to ensure that more decision-making about Scotland takes place in Scotland. It also facilitates the identification of Scottish priorities and the essential innovation or adaptation of policy to meet Scottish needs. The Government's commitment to this objective is founded on a belief that, while the whole of the United Kingdom should share similar policy goals, the different circumstances of each of its constituent parts mean that greater account in policy formation must be taken of the diversity which is the hallmark of these islands.

7.3   This Chapter outlines some of the steps which the Government propose to take to devolve more decision-making to Scotland.

TRAINING

7.4   The Government will take further steps towards greater policy and financial devolution to Scotland in the field of training. In particular the determination of future public expenditure provision for training programmes in Scotland will, from next year, become a matter solely for the Secretary of State for Scotland, with concomitant control over those policy matters where there is no need for full similarity and consistency of approach at a Great Britain level.

7.5   The keener awareness of the economic demands of local areas throughout Scotland which the creation of a network of local enterprise companies has generated has ensured that training programmes are better tailored to local needs. In view of this and in view of the other developments which have occurred in relation to Scottish Enterprise and Highlands and Islands Enterprise, the Government believe that there is now greater scope for the separate determination of training policy for Scotland. Accordingly, responsibility for determining training policy in Scotland will be transferred to the Secretary of State for Scotland as from 1 April 1994, within the framework of the overall strategic priorities, initiatives and policies developed by the Secretary of State for Employment in consultation with colleagues and collectively agreed.

INDUSTRIAL SUPPORT SCHEMES

7.6   The Department of Trade and Industry (DTI) at present has responsibility for a number of schemes to promote the introduction of new products and processes in industry, to undertake industrially relevant research and to facilitate the transfer of industrially relevant technologies from the science base. The Scottish Office Industry Department currently administers on the DTI's behalf 2 of the single company Research and Development schemes - SMART and SPUR - and Scottish Enterprise arranges for the delivery of the Consultancy Initiative, again on DTI's behalf. Funding for all three schemes is allocated from the DTI's budget and, in the case of SMART and SPUR, final approval for individual cases as well as responsibility for the administrative procedures rests with the DTI.

7.7   In the context of the policies emerging from the forthcoming White Paper on Science and Technology, the Government will review the scope for transferring from the Department of Trade and Industry to the Scottish Office Industry Department responsibility for a range of schemes for encouraging industrial innovation and technology transfer in Scotland. The object of the review will be to bring about transfer of responsibility wherever practicable.

HIGHLANDS AND ISLANDS AIRPORTS LTD

7.8   Highlands and Islands Airports Ltd (HIAL) is responsible for the management and operation of 8 airports in the Highlands and Islands of Scotland - Benbecula, Inverness, Islay, Kirkwall, Stornoway, Sumburgh, Tiree and Wick. These airports perform a vital social and economic function in the areas they serve. HIAL is at present a wholly-owned subsidiary of the Civil Aviation Authority (CAA), whose main responsibilities relate to the regulation of the air transport industry and the provision of national air traffic services.

7.9   It is proposed to transfer the ownership of HIAL from the CAA to the Secretary of State for Scotland. The Secretary of State is already responsible for paying deficit grant to HIAL in respect of the losses incurred in its airport operations, other than oil-related operations at Sumburgh. Bringing HIAL fully within the control of the Secretary of State will simplify the existing arrangements and provide that all strategic policy decisions regarding the company's operations as well as its financing are his responsibility. This will be of help to HIAL and in turn to those operators of air services using the company's airports, to the overall benefit of the areas serviced. Legislation to effect the transfer of ownership will be required.

SCOTTISH ARTS COUNCIL

7.10   Responsibility for the Scottish Arts Council at present rests with the Secretary of State for National Heritage. The Government believe that the body which supports the Arts in Scotland should be the responsibility of Scotland's Secretary of State and now propose to implement that change from 1 April 1994. The outstanding cultural development witnessed in Scotland in recent years is a tribute to the work of the SAC, among many others. The Government expect the Arts in Scotland, in partnership with the Secretary of

State for Scotland, to continue to go from strength to strength, displaying their cultural excellence within Scotland, in the rest of the UK and throughout the world.

RELOCATION

7.11   Scotland has benefited from the Government's policy of locating jobs away from London. Locations which have benefited are Falkirk, Glenrothes, Aberdeen, Edinburgh, Livingston, East Kilbride, Perth and Glasgow. In total over 4,000 civil service jobs are recorded as having been moved or being about to move to Scotland since 1979.

7.12   The Government recognise that Scotland is an attractive and appropriate location for the work of a number of Departments of Government, not just the Scottish Office. Where it is appropriate for other Departments to locate some of their work in Scotland, the Government will ensure that relocation is carried out.

7.13   The North Sea oil and gas industry works at the frontiers of technology and is a Scottish, and United Kingdom, success story. A significant number of private sector oil and gas companies have located their operations in Aberdeen, which is now the oil capital of Europe. The Government wish to match the private sector's commitment to Aberdeen. To do this, the Department of Trade and Industry will open a major new oil and gas office in Aberdeen. The office will provide key services, which until now have only been available from DTI headquarters in London, and will consist initially of some 60 staff, including both geologists and engineers as well as administrative support. This relocation confirms the Government's commitment to ensuring that Aberdeen continues to develop her rightful role as an international centre of the oil industry and further illustrates the qualities which Scotland has to offer as a location for Government activity.

CONCLUSION

7.14   The existence of her own Department, The Scottish Office, means that Scotland is already the home of much Government activity. But more can be done and the Government are keen to extend, where appropriate, the range of that activity carried out in Scotland.

7.15   The Government believe that the package of measures of administrative devolution outlined above amounts to a significant transfer of decision-making power from London to Scotland. This should enable policy-making for Scotland to reflect more accurately Scottish priorities and aspirations, in line with the Government's objectives. At the same time, the strong position within the Government as a whole of the Secretary of State for Scotland, his Ministers and his Department will be considerably strengthened when these transfers are put into effect, making them better able to exert even more influence on behalf of Scotland over a wider range of policy.

7.16   But the existence of The Scottish Office should not preclude the extension of other Departments' activities in Scotland. Scotland has a contribution to make to the government of the United Kingdom as a whole and some of that contribution can be made from Scotland. With many outstanding qualities, Scotland is an attractive location for both civil service posts and European institutions. The new DTI office in Aberdeen is just one example of this. When and where relocation reviews are being undertaken, the Government will take full account of the numerous advantages which Scotland offers as a location.

CHAPTER 8
THE WAY AHEAD: RESPONSIVE GOVERNMENT

It is important that concern with improving the procedures of Parliament and the structures of Government machinery does not lead us to ignore issues concerned with the more fundamental relationships between Government and people in Scotland. Tackling those issues calls for a more visibly responsive Scottish Office. Far too few Scots know even of the existence of The Scottish Office, which is their Department in the Government. The Government are determined to remedy this situation.

8.2   The Government have published since 1991 a Departmental Report entitled "Serving Scotland's Needs" (Cm 2214) which sets out the Secretary of State's public expenditure plans together with information on past achievements and current policy objectives of The Scottish Office and Associated Departments. "Serving Scotland's Needs" is a substantial and detailed document of record which serves a particular need for a specialised readership. In addition, however, and in keeping with the Citizen's Charter, the Government intend to proceed in due course with the publication of a concise and accessible Annual Report on the activities of The Scottish Office, the Non-Departmental Public Bodies and the Next Steps Agencies which are the responsibility of the Secretary of State. The Annual Report will record the activities and achievements of the preceding year, as well as any difficulties encountered, and will set targets, aims and objectives to be met in the following year.

8.3   Once this new approach is up and running the Government will ensure that there is an early opportunity for the Annual Report to be referred to the Scottish Grand Committee, where its contents can be scrutinised and debated by Scottish Members of Parliament.

8.4   Although The Scottish Office has offices in every region and island area in the country, the Departments of the Secretary of State for Scotland are located predominantly in and around Edinburgh. The Government are keen to see a broader spread of Scottish Office locations around the country and will seek opportunities for further dispersal, both of parts of The Scottish Office and of non-departmental public bodies for which the Secretary of State is responsible. The Government will examine in particular the division of responsibility between headquarters and local organisations and the scope for locating new units and bodies outside the Edinburgh and Glasgow areas where there is a sound financial and operational case for doing so. Plans are already afoot in Historic Scotland to introduce more decentralisation to area offices in Stirling, Fort George and outer Edinburgh. Scottish Natural Heritage has set up area offices in Inverness, Aberdeen, Riccarton (near Edinburgh) and Clydebank.

8.5 The Government also wish to take steps to make The Scottish Office more accessible to the general public throughout Scotland. The Government will explore ways of improving the dialogue between The Scottish Office and the public it exists to serve by making information about its responsibilities and the services it provides more readily available and by providing better opportunities of access for members of the public to make enquiries, register complaints or offer comments and suggestions about policies or services. The Government will establish a central enquiry unit, accessible from all parts of Scotland for the cost of a local telephone call, which will allow the public to make contact with The Scottish Office and be put in touch with the member of staff dealing with the issue of concern to them. Where the issue in question is the responsibility of another Government department, The Scottish Office will assist the caller in identifying the correct source of information.

8.6 The new central enquiry unit of the Scottish Office will be backed up by the designation of many of the existing Departmental offices around Scotland as Scottish Office information points. This initiative will heighten the visibility and accessibility of The Scottish Office in most of the main towns and cities in Scotland. This will enable individuals or groups to obtain much more easily information about Scottish Office activity and policy. These new arrangements will provide an extensive network of information points around Scotland to support the central enquiry unit.

8.7 The Government will examine the case for supplementing these Scottish Office information points with other information points in smaller towns around Scotland, operated on an agency basis by, for example, solicitors, accountants and other professionals. These agents would provide the public with a contact point and information service in towns where The Scottish Office does not have a presence.

8.8 The Government hope to have the initiatives outlined in this Chapter in place as quickly as possible. They will be kept under constant review to ensure that they meet the needs of the Scottish people. The Scottish Office has much to offer the people of Scotland. As well as representing their interests within the Government of the United Kingdom, the Scottish Office is a source of useful advice and information. It should be more visible and more accessible. These initiatives will make it so and that, in turn, will make the Scottish Office more responsive.

CHAPTER 9
THE WAY AHEAD: POWER TO THE CITIZEN

The Government are deeply committed in principle to the diffusion of power. In their drive to devolve more decision-making power to Scotland and within Scotland, the Government will continually seek ways of extending choice and opportunity in such a way as to enable the people of Scotland to have more say over their own lives. Enabling Scots to have more real decision-making power in their own hands is at the heart of the Government's strategy for the future. The Government wish to confer more real rights on ordinary Scots.

9.2   As a result, individuals will have more opportunity to exercise real choice. Further extensions of ownership will help to achieve this objective and the vigorous application of Citizen's Charter principles across the range of public services will enable Scots to secure the high standards in these services to which they are entitled. When the Prime Minister launched the Citizen's Charter White Paper in 1991 he described the Charter as being about giving more power to the citizen through being better informed about rights and entitlements, better able to exercise choice and better able to secure redress when things go wrong. The development of the Charter and its related initiatives will mean more power is put directly into the hands of Scottish people than ever before. It will both define and advance the position of the Scottish citizen in relation to public bodies.

9.3   The White Paper "The Citizen's Charter: First Report 1992" (Cm 2101) gives a full account of the progress that has been made in Scotland in the last year. The Scottish Office will play a central role in driving further forward the Citizen's Charter initiative in Scotland. This will apply in relation both to the services The Scottish Office provides direct to the public and to the very important public services it funds and sponsors. The programme of reform is an ambitious one.

9.4   Within the next few months the Government will bring forward a number of wide-ranging new initiatives. A Further and Higher Education Charter for Scotland, spelling out the standards students can expect from the institutions at which they study, will be published, as will a Householder's Guide to Planning in Scotland. A Charter detailing the rights of the citizen in regard to local authority environmental services of most immediate concern to him or her is also being prepared for publication and a Guide setting out the rights of private sector tenants in Scotland will be released soon. The Inspectorates of some of Scotland's key public services – police, schools and social work – will be strengthened by the appointment of lay inspectors, and their reports will be published. For example, the

Government will shortly publish a consultation document on the Social Work Services Inspectorate. It will outline the developments the Government intends for the future, and will emphasise the key feature of all effective inspection – its independence. But these initiatives, while important in themselves, are just part of the Government's strategy to codify and strengthen more comprehensively than ever before the rights of the Scottish citizen.

9.5   The Government also want to shift decision-making, where practicable, to Scotland's local communities. The Government recognise, and welcome, the fact that there is in Scotland a stronger sense of community than is sometimes felt elsewhere. Scotland is a diverse country and requires the sensitive handling of policy issues. The Government are therefore committed to devolving more decision-making not only to Scotland, but within Scotland, too.

9.6   This process has already started, for example, with the establishment of local enterprise companies (LECs). The progressive handover of greater responsibilities to LECs will continue, building upon the package of increased flexibilities introduced this financial year. In addition, from next year there will be increased discretion for Scottish Enterprise, Highlands and Islands Enterprise and LECs to determine the allocation among activities of their programme funding from Government grant-in-aid, while retaining the broad control of the division between training and non-training activities.

9.7   The creation of parent-led School Boards facilitated a reassertion of parental influence over schools. The Government believe that schools play a central part in the life of every community and, indeed, encourage that sense of community. The introduction of devolved school management over the next few years will ensure there is more local decision-making at school level where parents can more easily contribute; and the establishment of NHS Trusts throughout Scotland is giving responsibility for running local hospitals back to local people.

9.8   The Secretary of State is responsible for making appointments to a large number of public bodies throughout Scotland. Many of these bodies have been established as a consequence of the Government's drive to devolve decision-making to the lowest level. The Secretary of State is committed to selecting names from more diverse backgrounds and experience and to appointing individuals who reflect local interests. He is now taking active steps to consult more widely about public appointments, and this will continue.

9.9   The Government's plans for the reform of local government are at the heart of their strategy to pass decision-making downwards. The new single-tier, all-purpose local authorities will be better able to promote effectively the interests of the area they represent. They will be able to identify more with their area. And they will be more accountable to the people who live there. In sum, they will reflect the diversity of Scotland as a whole and revive the dynamism of local democracy.

CONCLUSION

9.10   A key theme for the future will be to place decision-taking closer to the point where services are delivered. While it will take time to ensure that Citizen's Charter principles take root everywhere, the process is now well under way. No-one should now be unaware of his or her rights and entitlements. The Government are engaged in a determined drive to extend more power to the Scottish people. This will in time result in the redefinition of the relationship between the Scottish citizen and the previously too remote state. Over the next few years the people of Scotland will be empowered to take more decisions affecting their own lives than ever before in modern times. The result will be an increasing number of clearly defined rights for each Scottish citizen, each meeting important and identifiable needs. That truly will put power in the hands of the Scottish citizen.

CHAPTER 10
BRINGING THE UNION ALIVE

The proposals in this White Paper will all contribute in one way or another to improving the governance of Scotland and strengthening Scotland's place in the United Kingdom. In this and other ways the Government seek to bring the Union alive.

10.2   As a first step the Government will put renewed emphasis on the fact that the Union matters, not just to Scotland but to the whole of the United Kingdom. The Union is not something which affects just one Department of Government, The Scottish Office. If new life is to be breathed into the Union its existence must permeate every area of government. Account must be taken of the Union by all Government Departments, at all times. The national celebration of the Millenium will create a good opportunity to re-emphasise the importance of the Union for us all. The Millenium Fund - to be created from part of the proceeds of the National Lottery - will foster the sense of Union by funding major projects in all parts of the United Kingdom.

10.3   And if the Union is to flourish in the future a more concerted recognition of Scotland's status as a nation will be necessary. It should be a mark of Scotland's self-confidence in her own status as a nation that she shares her sovereignty with the other parts of the United Kingdom. But the willingness to share that sovereignty must never be taken for granted.

10.4   This White Paper indicates some of the ways in which such recognition can be given. But there are others. For example, there should be more acknowledgement from all parts of the United Kingdom of the significance of the major institutions of Scottish life - the legal system, the professions, the Churches, the Universities, the learned societies and the financial institutions - and of Scottish cultural excellence and the arts. Scottish pride in these should be shared by the rest of the United Kingdom and their distinctive features should be promoted abroad.

10.5   Parliament in Westminster is the Parliament of the whole of the United Kingdom. It is at the heart of our democracy and its Members enjoy equal rights, regardless of which part of the United Kingdom they represent. The Government remains committed to ensuring that it is seen as fully a United Kingdom Parliament, reflecting in its composition, institutions and ceremonial, the diversity of the Kingdom's constituent parts.

10.6   We should not hesitate to create, when appropriate, new bodies to take account of the distinctive Scottish identity. Sometimes such organisations will be in the public sector, such as Scottish Natural Heritage. On other occasions they will belong to the private sector, such as Scottish Power. In either instance the case for establishing new Scottish institutions will be closely examined.

10.7   The Union, far from diminishing Scotland, has in fact allowed the development of a stronger Scottish identity shaped, as it is, by Scotland's place in the United Kingdom and in the wider world. That such a development has taken place since 1707 is a tribute to the nature of the Union and the way in which it avoids imposing uniformity throughout these islands. But the strength of Scottish identity poses a challenge to government: to respect and cherish the differences between each of the constituent parts of the United Kingdom. Fundamental to that is a need to recognise the individual needs of each and to respond sensitively to them.

10.8   Government in Scotland must be more visible because if government is invisible the benefits of the Union may become so too. The proposals contained in this White Paper are designed to improve the visibility of government in Scotland but there are other things which can be done.

10.9   Scotland should be the home of more government activity. Edinburgh is a capital city within the United Kingdom and as such is an eminently suitable venue for a range of government activities. The city recently took her place on the world stage as the venue for the European Council. The Government will seek to ensure that other important state and government events take place in Scotland.

10.10   Ways must be found of ensuring that Scotland plays a bigger part in the United Kingdom as a whole. One of the advantages of the Union is that it enables each of the constituent parts to be more outward-looking. There are a number of ways in which this may be done and not all of them are within the Government's power to achieve. But one area the Government will be looking at closely is the continued appointment of Scots to public bodies covering the whole of the United Kingdom and to see whether further improvement might be made.

10.11   The people of Scotland rightly aspire to a special place for their country within the United Kingdom and throughout the wider world. At the same time they want their Scottishness to be recognised, understood and respected. The Union must be flexible enough to take account of this and to ensure that Scottish aspirations are met and distinctive Scottish qualities recognised. It is the Government's task to ensure this, and through the proposals in this White Paper the Government intend to achieve it.

10.12   Renewal of the Union may not happen overnight. But over a period of time the Government believe that these measures and others which will emerge will, when combined with a sensitive and sensible approach to the governance of Scotland, bring the Union alive.

10.13   The Union is a partnership of peoples. It is a partnership that has evolved over time. An enduring and adaptable partnership, it has stood Scotland, and the other parts of the United Kingdom, in good stead. But all partnerships require reassessment from time to time, and the Union is no exception. This White Paper marks the start of a continuing reappraisal by the Government of the way the Union works and of how it can be improved. If there emerge over time other measures that would strengthen Scotlands place in the Union, the Government will consider them. Thus, this White Paper is not the culmination of a process, but the commencement.

10.14   The Government believe that the Union has been good for Scotland and that Scotland has been good for the Union. It is a partnership which has endured, and matured, and will continue to do so. It is, above all, a partnership for good.

SCOTTISH OFFICE MINISTERS AND THEIR RESPONSIBILITIES

MINISTER OF STATE

THE RT. HON THE LORD FRASER OF CARMYLLIE QC
Minister for Health and Home Affairs

The Scottish Office Home and Health Department
Health Policy and Public Health;
NHS Management Executive, Health Boards and Common Services Agency,
Hospital Services, General Practitioner Services (Doctors, Dentists, Chemists and Opticians),
Community Health Services, Ambulance Service and Health Education;
Social Work Services.

Police and Fire Services; Civil Law and Criminal Justice;
Civil Defence and Civil Emergencies; Prisons; Superannuation; General Register Office (Scotland);
Scottish Courts Administration;
Scottish Record Office; Registers of Scotland.

Central Services
Constitutional Matters; Women's Issues.

Spokesman - House of Lords, on all Scottish Affairs.

PARLIAMENTARY UNDER SECRETARIES OF STATE

LORD JAMES DOUGLAS-HAMILTON MP
Minister for Education and Housing

The Scottish Office Education Department
Education – Including Primary, Secondary, Further and Higher Education;
Youth and Community Services.

The Scottish Office Environment Department
Housing; Building Control; Construction Industry.

The Scottish Office Industry Department
Roads and Transport; Urban Policy;
Highlands and Islands Enterprise; Scottish Tourist Board;
Co-ordination of Government action in relation to the Highlands and Islands.

Spokesman - House of Commons, on Home Affairs.

MR. J. ALLAN STEWART MP
Minister for Industry and Local Government

The Scottish Office Industry Department
Industrial and Regional Development; Scottish Enterprise; Training;
Energy; New Towns.

The Scottish Office Environment Department
Local Government and Local Government Finance;
Town and Country Planning.

Spokesman - House of Commons, on Health and Social Work.

SIR HECTOR MONRO MP
Minister for Agriculture and the Environment

The Scottish Office Agriculture and Fisheries Department
Agriculture, Fisheries, Scottish Fisheries Protection Agency; Scottish Agricultural
Science Agency.

The Scottish Office Education Department
The Arts; Museums and Libraries; Sport and Recreation.

The Scottish Office Environment Department
Water, Sewerage and Pollution; Historic Scotland; Natural Heritage; Co-ordination of
Rural Affairs.

Forestry Commission
Forestry.

MINISTERIAL COMMITTEES WITH SCOTTISH OFFICE MEMBERSHIP

The names and terms of reference of standing Ministerial Committees, Sub-Committees and Working Groups of which the Secretary of State for Scotland is a member. (In addition the Secretary of State would be invited to attend meetings of certain other Committees as and when the business required.)

MINISTERIAL COMMITTEE ON ECONOMIC AND DOMESTIC POLICY (EDP)

Terms of Reference:

"To consider strategic issues relating to the Government's economic and domestic policies".

MINISTERIAL COMMITTEE ON SCIENCE AND TECHNOLOGY (EDS)

Terms of Reference:

"To review science and technology policy".

MINISTERIAL COMMITTEE ON INDUSTRIAL, COMMERCIAL AND CONSUMER AFFAIRS (EDI)

Terms of Reference:

"To consider industrial, commercial, and consumer issues, including questions of competition and deregulation".

MINISTERIAL COMMITTEE ON THE ENVIRONMENT (EDE)

Terms of Reference:

"To consider questions of environmental policy."

MINISTERIAL COMMITTEE ON HOME AND SOCIAL AFFAIRS (EDH)

Terms of Reference:

"To consider home and social policy issues".

MINISTERIAL COMMITTEE ON LOCAL GOVERNMENT (EDL)

Terms of Reference:

"To consider issues affecting local government, including the annual allocation of resources".

MINISTERIAL COMMITTEE ON LEGISLATION (LG)

The Lord Advocate is also a member of this Committee.

Terms of Reference:

"To examine all draft Bills; to consider the Parliamentary handling of Government Bills, European Community documents and Private Members' business, and such other related matters as may be necessary; and to keep under review the Government's policy in relation to issues of Parliamentary procedures".

MINISTERIAL COMMITTEE ON CIVIL SERVICE PAY (EDC)

Terms of Reference:

"To determine the basis of the annual negotiations and consider other matters concerning civil service pay".

MINISTERIAL SUB-COMMITTEE ON HEALTH STRATEGY (EDH(H))

Terms of Reference:

"To oversee the development, implementation and monitoring of the Government's Health Strategy, to coordinate the Government's policies on United Kingdom-wide issues affecting health, and report as necessary to the Ministerial Committee on Home and Social Affairs".

MINISTERIAL SUB-COMMITTEE ON PUBLIC SECTOR PAY (EDI(P))

Terms of Reference:

"To coordinate the handling of pay issues in the public sector, and report as necessary to the Ministerial Committee on Industrial, Commercial and Consumer Affairs".

MINISTERIAL SUB-COMMITTEE ON EUROPEAN QUESTIONS (OPD(E))

Terms of Reference:

"To consider questions relating to the United Kingdom's membership of the European Community and to report as necessary to the Ministerial Committee on Defence and Overseas Policy."

MINISTERIAL SUB-COMMITTEE ON TERRORISM (OPD(T))

Terms of Reference:

"To keep under review the arrangements for countering terrorism and for dealing with terrorist incidents and their consequences and to report as necessary to the Ministerial Committee on Defence and Overseas Policy."

The names and terms of reference of Ministerial Sub-Committees on which the Minister of State or a Parliamentary Under-Secretary of State is a member.

MINISTERIAL SUB-COMMITTEE ON DRUG MISUSE (EDH(D))

Terms of Reference:

"To coordinate the Government's national and international policies for tackling drugs misuse, and report as necessary to the Ministerial Committee on Home and Social Affairs".

MINISTERIAL SUB-COMMITTEE ON COORDINATION OF URBAN POLICY (EDH(U))

Terms of Reference:

"To monitor and coordinate Government action on inner cities, and report as necessary to the Ministerial Committee on Home and Social Affairs".

MINISTERIAL SUB-COMMITTEE ON ALCOHOL MISUSE (EDH(A))

Terms of Reference:

"To review and develop the Government's strategy for combating the misuse of alcohol and to oversee its continuing implementation, and report as necessary to the Ministerial Committee on Home and Social Affairs".

MINISTERIAL SUB-COMMITTEE ON WOMEN'S ISSUES (EDH(W))

Terms of Reference:

"To review and develop the Government's policy and strategy on issues of special concern to women; to oversee their implementation; and to report as necessary to the Ministerial Committee on Home and Social Affairs".

MINISTERIAL GROUP ON REFUGEES FROM FORMER YUGOSLAVIA (GEN 24)

Terms of Reference:

"To consider whether a visa regime should be instituted for citizens of former Yugoslavia in the context of the Government's overall policy towards that region and to review the practical arrangements for the reception and subsequent support of those arriving in the United Kingdom from this area taking account of the implications for the treatment of refugees from other parts of the world, and to report to Cabinet".

In addition the Lord Advocate is a member of the following Committee:

MINISTERIAL COMMITTEE ON THE QUEEN'S SPEECHES AND FUTURE LEGISTRATION (FLG)

Terms of Reference:

"To propose and submit to the Cabinet drafts of The Queen's Speeches to Parliament, and proposals for the Government's legislation programme for each Session of Parliament".

THE SECRETARY OF STATE'S DEPARTMENTS

THE SCOTTISH OFFICE

1.　As mentioned in Chapter 5, the Secretary of State's responsibilities are administered by 5 main departments (which include 3 executive agencies). These departments are:

> The Scottish Office Agriculture and Fisheries Department;

> The Scottish Office Education Department;

> The Scottish Office Environment Department;

> The Scottish Office Home and Health Department; and

> The Scottish Office Industry Department.

Together with Central Services, embracing support services such as the Office of the Solicitor to the Secretary of State, The Scottish Office Information Directorate, the Finance and Personnel Groups and the Directorate of Administrative Services, these departments are collectively known as The Scottish Office.

ASSOCIATED DEPARTMENTS

2.　In addition the Secretary of State has some degree of responsibility for a number of other Scottish departments including the Scottish Courts Administration, the General Register Office for Scotland and the Scottish Record Office; and for another executive agency, the Registers of Scotland.

GB STATUTORY BODIES

3.　The Secretary of State also bears ministerial responsibilities for the activities in Scotland of several statutory bodies whose functions extend throughout Great Britain, such as the Intervention Board Executive Agency, which implements in the United Kingdom the market support measures of the EC Common Agricultural Policy.

THE FUNCTIONS OF THE 5 MAIN SCOTTISH OFFICE DEPARTMENTS
THE SCOTTISH OFFICE AGRICULTURE AND FISHERIES DEPARTMENT (SOAFD)

4.　SOAFD:

> -promotes agriculture and fisheries in Scotland;

-advises and supports the Secretary of State in his capacity as one of the 4 UK Agriculture and Fisheries Ministers;

-is responsible for food safety matters in Scotland;

-participates both at UK and EC level in the management of the Common Agricultural Policy and the Common Fisheries Policy as they affect Scottish interests and in the negotiation of the further development of both of these policies;

-oversees support arrangements for agricultural commodities and other assistance to producers;

-is responsible for 2 agencies - the Scottish Agricultural Science Agency and the Scottish Fisheries Protection Agency; and

-gives assistance to the agricultural and fishing industries by sponsoring relevant research.

The amount planned for programmes administered by SOAFD for 1993-94 is £441 million as set out in the Departmental Report "Serving Scotland's Needs". (More information about planned public expenditure for SOAFD and other Scottish Office departments can be found in this publication.) To carry out these functions SOAFD has 1459 staff, including 413 employed in the 2 agencies.

Some **specific current objectives** for SOAFD include:

-successfully implementing the Common Agriculture Policy reform measures and evaluating their impact;

-embedding environmental protection conditions into the main agricultural support schemes;

-establishing a successful Scottish Food Group to help promote Scottish agricultural exports;

-recovering through conservation and structural measures a more healthy state of white fish stocks;

-ensuring that a new EC Multi-Annual Guidance Programme on Fleet size is determined with proper regard to the interests of the Scottish fishing industry; and

-implementing and operating adequate measures to implement EC and UK legislation on food safety and to ensure that speedy and effective action is taken in response to food hazards.

THE SCOTTISH OFFICE EDUCATION DEPARTMENT (SOED)

5.   SOED:

-advises and assists the Secretary of State in exercise of his functions and responsibilities in relation to education, the arts and sport in Scotland;

-provides policy objectives and, where appropriate, establishes standards for the performance of these services;

-provides an appropriate framework of primary and secondary legislation as well as guidelines and advice to enable these objectives and standards to be achieved;

-monitors the effectiveness of the provision of services by local authorities and public and voluntary bodies;

-provides financial support for the provision of the services by bodies other than local authorities;

-determines the appropriate levels of local authority expenditure on these services for the purposes of the aggregate exchequer funding settlement and capital expenditure control; and

-makes provision for funding systems for further and higher education and a system of support for students in full-time higher education.

The amount planned for programmes administered by SOED for 1993-94 is £1,236 million, with the largest share (£1,182 million) allocated to education. To carry out these functions, SOED has some 492 staff.

Some **specific current objectives** for SOED include:

-improving the quality of education for pupils aged 5-14 by providing national guidance on the curriculum and on assessment, the latter supported by an effective system of national testing;

-delivering the various commitments included in the Parents' Charter, particularly those related to the provision of information;

-promoting the option of self governing schools;

-improving the quality of further education and its management;

-increasing participation by Scottish students in higher education;

-developing a coherent and flexible system of vocational qualifications;

-conducting a review of Gaelic language education; and

-working with football authorities in improving standards of crowd behaviour and safety.

THE SCOTTISH OFFICE ENVIRONMENT DEPARTMENT (SOEnvD)

6.   SOEnvD:

-advises the Secretary of State on environmental protection policy and related matters, standards of control over air, land and waste pollution and the regulation of waste disposal, including radioactive waste;

-advises the Secretary of State on policy and issues affecting nature conservation and promoting conservation and enjoyment of the countryside including sponsorship of Scottish Natural Heritage;

-co-ordinates Scottish Office policy on rural areas including advice to the Secretary of State on issues affecting land use, in particular forestry, leisure and recreation and rural settlements and buildings;

-maintains the statutory planning framework and advises the Secretary of State on policy and on cases which he has to determine;

-promotes effective provision of water supplies, sewerage, flood prevention and coastal protection;

-through the agency, Historic Scotland, promotes the conservation and public enjoyment of Scotland's ancient monuments, sites, historic buildings, parks and gardens;

-advances and administers the Government's housing policies for public and private sectors including the sponsorship of Scottish Homes;

-administers the Government's policies on structure, organisation, finance and procedures for local government; and

-is responsible for building control, building advice and support, civil engineering and the provision of statistical services to other Scottish departments.

The amount planned for programmes administered by SOEnvD in 1993-94 is £974 million, £632 million of which is planned for the housing programme. SOEnvD is also responsible for administering central Government non-hypothecated support to Scottish local authorities' current expenditure; planned provision in 1993-94 is £4,857 million. SOEnvD has 1,213 staff, including 693 working in Historic Scotland.

Some **specific current objectives** for SOEnvD include:

-achieving higher levels of home ownership through specific measures such as improvements in the Right to Buy Scheme and through the work of Scottish Homes, including the promotion of low cost home ownership and the encouragement of housing co-operatives;

-promoting diversity and competition in the provision and management of rented housing;

-promoting improvement in housing quality;

-developing a more integrated and effective system of pollution control by establishing a single Scottish Environment Protection Agency;

-overseeing the introduction of all 8 parts of the Environmental Protection Act 1990;

-securing the orderly introduction of the council tax on 1 April 1993;

-continuing consultations and making preparation for legislation on the reform of local government structure;

-working through Scottish Natural Heritage to achieve objectives for nature conservation and the countryside in Scotland; and

-promoting the care of all nationally important monuments.

THE SCOTTISH OFFICE HOME AND HEALTH DEPARTMENT (SOHHD)

7. SOHHD carries out home, health and social work functions.

On the Home side, it is responsible for:

-the Scottish police, prison and fire services, civil defence and emergency planning;

-policy on civil and criminal law, including advising the Secretary of State on parole, life sentence prisoners and case work on alleged miscarriages of justices;

-the management of the Scottish Prison Service;

-dealing with certain royal, church and ceremonial matters; and

-seeking to improve the economy, efficiency and effectiveness of the police, prison and fire services through its Inspectorates.

On the Health side it is responsible for:

-policy on health and on health services in Scotland (including co-ordination of policies to improve public health);

-the management of the National Health Service in Scotland and securing improvements in its delivery of service and in value for money.

The Department is also responsible for:

-advising and assisting the Secretary of State in the exercise of his functions in relation to Social Work in Scotland; and

-the regulation, management and payment of certain public sector pensions.

To enable SOHHD to meet its objectives, the amount planned for programmes in 1993-94 is £4,443 million, composed of £602 million for law and order and protective services, £3,766 million for health and £75 million for social work. The Department has 863 staff, plus a further 4,577 in the Scottish Prison Service and its Headquarters.

Some **specific current objectives** for SOHHD include:

For Home Affairs

-formulating legislative proposals to improve the efficiency and effectiveness of the Scottish criminal justice system and identifying strategies to help reduce offending, particularly by young people;

-implementing the reform of the law of Bankruptcy in Scotland to secure greater value for money and reduce the burden on the taxpayer;

-reviewing the effectiveness of the legal aid system and implementing agreed changes;

-co-ordinating and strengthening value for money policies in the police service and promoting effective crime prevention; and

-improving the quality of service provided by the Scottish Prison Service through a programme of prisoner focused initiatives and management change; and establishing the Service as an executive agency from April 1993.

For Health and Social Work:

-improving the health of the people of Scotland, for example by action to reduce the rate of premature death, through health education and health promotion initiatives;

-combating the misuse of alcohol, tobacco and drugs;

-working with Health Boards and the Common Services Agency to achieve high standards of health care and to ensure that the services delivered meet people's needs, respect their individuality, and represent value for money;

-ensuring that optimum use is made of resources throughout the NHS and, in particular, that the NHS retains and develops the commitment of staff, who are its most valuable resource;

-carrying through the implementation of the changes in the NHS provided for in the NHS and Community Care Act 1990, including the establishment of further NHS Trusts and the expansion of GP fundholding;

-following up the review of child care law and preparing a White Paper on Child Care Policy in preparation for Child Care legislation; and

-reducing the numbers who might otherwise go to prison by developing the quality of social work services for offenders.

THE SCOTTISH OFFICE INDUSTRY DEPARTMENT (SOID)

8.   SOID:

-is responsible for the development of enterprise in Scotland;

-gives financial and/or advisory support, directly and through sponsored bodies, for competitive firms, entrepreneurship, inward investment, exporting and training;

-seeks to ensure that the markets in land and capital are meeting the needs of new or expanding enterprise;

-supervises the work of Scottish Enterprise, Highlands and Islands Enterprise and the new town development corporations, while maintaining a general co-ordinating role in relation to the Government's policies in and for the Highlands and Islands;

-supports urban regeneration;

-supports tourism through the Scottish Tourist Board;

-secures the building and maintenance of the trunk road system;

-allocates resources for local authority roads and transport systems;

-promotes road safety;

-supports a number of strategic shipping and air routes in the Highlands and Islands and sponsors Caledonian MacBrayne;

-co-ordinates The Scottish Office's general interest in European Community matters not otherwise allocated and secures assistance to appropriate areas from European structural funds;

-is responsible for the Government's residual interest in the privatised Scottish Power Plc and Scottish Hydro-Electric Plc, and sponsors Scottish Nuclear Ltd;

-gives economic advice to Ministers and certain other departments of The Scottish Office.

To fulfil these and other objectives, the amount planned for programmes administered by SOID in 1993-94 is £1,204 million, of which £530 million is allocated for industry, energy, trade and employment and £406 million set aside for roads and transport. The department has 572 staff.

Some **specific current objectives** for SOID include:

-the development of a better targeted regional policy as a result of the completion of the current review of the Assisted Area Maps;

-improving Scotland's export performance through Scottish Trade International in partnership with Scottish Enterprise;

-delivery of the CBI's training targets in Scotland;

-upgrading the road network, with particular attention to investment in strategic routes of economic importance;

-reducing the level of Scottish roads casualties within the general government framework of reducing casualties by one-third by the year 2000; and

-making substantial progress in physical, economic and social terms in all 4 Scottish Office led urban partnership areas.

EXECUTIVE AGENCIES: THE "NEXT STEPS" INITIATIVE

9.   The Next Steps Initiative launched in 1988 is intended to improve management in the civil service and the efficiency and quality of services provided to the public and to customers within government. This has involved setting up, as far as practicable, separate units or agencies to perform the executive functions of government.

10.   The **Scottish Agricultural Science Agency** was established as an agency from 1 April 1992, bringing to 4 the number of agencies solely within the responsibilities of the Secretary of State. The others are the **Registers of Scotland**, established on 1 April 1990,

and **Historic Scotland** and the **Scottish Fisheries Protection Agency**, both established on 1 April 1991.

11.   Three further candidates for agency status have been announced, the **Scottish Office Pensions Agency**, the **Scottish Prison Service** and the **Scottish Record Office**. They are due to be launched as agencies on 1 April 1993. Further candidates will be brought forward later.

12.   These agencies are freestanding and each carries out specific activities. Each agency is headed by a Chief Executive, who is directly accountable to a Minister. The Chief Executives are set targets for financial performance and quality of service, and have financial and management freedoms tailored to help them do the job better. The details of these arrangements are set out clearly in the framework documents which are drawn up for each agency.

13.   All agencies are fully accountable to Parliament through the Secretary of State. The "Next Steps" initiative has also enhanced accountability to Parliament through its requirement for agencies to publish their framework documents, annual targets, annual reports and accounts and, where appropriate, their corporate and business plans. This means that Agency Chief Executives are answerable to the Public Accounts Committee for the use of resources allocated to them.

14.   While remaining part of the Civil Service, and accountable to Parliament through the Secretary of State, agencies benefit from the clarification of role and enhanced corporate identity which are essential features of "Next Steps" and from increased flexibilities, particularly in the fields of personnel and finance.

NON DEPARTMENTAL PUBLIC BODIES (NDPBS)

15.   Non-Department Public Bodies (NDPBs) are organisations which cover a broad spectrum of activities and include Scottish Homes, Scottish Enterprise, the Local Government Boundary Commission for Scotland and Children's Panels. They have a role in the processes of central government but they are not themselves Scottish Office Departments. NDPBs for the most part are separate legal entities with a considerable degree of policy and operational freedom and independence and the Minister is not accountable in the same way to Parliament for their activities. There are 3 categories of NDPBs:-

Executive Bodies

These are bodies with executive, administrative, regulatory or commercial functions. Generally described as executive NDPBs, they normally employ staff and have their own budget. They usually carry out prescribed functions but the degree of their operational independence varies. Scottish Homes and Scottish Enterprise are classed as executive NDPBs.

Advisory Bodies

This group consists mainly of bodies (other than committees of officials) set up by the Secretary of State which advise Ministers and their departments on particular matters. The Local Government Boundary Commission for Scotland falls into this category. Generally, advisory NDPBs do not employ staff or incur expenditure on their own account.

Tribunals

These are bodies whose functions, like those of courts of law, are essentially judicial, eg Children's Panels. They include bodies which have licensing and appeal functions and they are independent of the executive.

16.   The relationship between Scottish NDPBs and The Scottish Office is clearly defined for each body in a way which supports the appropriate degree of delegation and independence of the NDPB. At the same time their financial management arrangements must ensure propriety, regularity and value for money. Further information about NDPBs sponsored by The Scottish Office, including appointments, staffing and funding, is contained in the publication "Public Bodies" which is produced annually and published by HMSO.

OTHER GOVERNMENT DEPARTMENTS

SCOTTISH COURTS ADMINISTRATION

17.   This Department provides on behalf of the Secretary of State, and in co-operation with the Judiciary, the central organisation and administration required for the running of the Scottish Courts (other than District Courts and certain Tribunals). It also advises and assists the Lord Advocate in the exercise of his ministerial responsibilities. This covers the general oversight of certain branches of Scots law dealing with Courts and Tribunals, and the administration of justice. **Specific objectives currently include** the reduction of court delays, securing effective implementation of law reform measures; and improving the services given by court staff, including the information and facilities for citizens using the Scottish Courts.

THE SCOTTISH RECORD OFFICE

18.   The function of the Scottish Record Office (SRO) is to act as the repository for the public records of Scotland and other records deposited within it for permanent preservation. **SRO's aims include** the provision of sufficient archival accommodation for present and future record holdings and the improvement of services to Departments, the legal profession and the public.

THE GENERAL REGISTER OFFICE FOR SCOTLAND

19.   The main functions of this Department are to administer registration of events such as births, deaths, marriages, divorces and adoption and to administer the statutes relating to the formalities of marriage and conduct of civil marriage. It takes periodic censuses of Scotland's population and prepares and publishes demographic and other statistics for the purposes of both general government, including medical research, and the private sector. It also makes available public records about individuals to customers and maintains for The Scottish Office the National Health Service Central Register of Patients. GRO(S) seeks to ensure that information collected is relevant, accurate, complete and updated as required, to give ready access to public records and to produce relevant statistics to meet customers' needs at reasonable prices.

REGISTERS OF SCOTLAND

20.   Registers of Scotland is an executive agency responsible for maintaining certain public registers. These provide for the registration of deeds relating to rights in land, as

well as a wide range of deeds relating to succession, trusts, family agreements, diligence and sequestration, state appointments and others. The maintenance of the 2 largest registers of interest in land in Scotland, the General Register of Sasines and Land Register, requires the application of most of the resources of the Agency. **Specific current objectives include** improving the effectiveness of service delivery, extending the operation of the Land Register to include more counties and monitoring customer satisfaction.

THE FORESTRY COMMISSION

21.   This functions as a Government Department with responsibilities for forestry throughout Great Britain. It reports to Forestry Ministers, namely the Secretary of State for Scotland (who takes the lead role), the Minister of Agriculture, Fisheries and Food and the Secretary of State for Wales. It is responsible for advising Ministers on forestry policy and for the implementation of that policy.

The aims of the Government's forestry policy are:

> -to facilitate the sustainable management of Britain's existing woods and forests; and

> -to encourage a steady expansion of tree cover to increase the many, diverse benefits that forests provide.

Current objectives include prevention of woodland loss, expanding the forest area, securing environmental benefits and encouraging greater access to, and recreational use of, forests.

THE SCOTTISH OFFICE AND ASSOCIATED DEPARTMENTS

STAFF IN POST[1]

Agriculture and Fisheries[2]	1,459
Education	492
Environment[3]	1,213
Home and Health[4]	5,440
Industry	572
Central Services	1,523
The Scottish Office Total	10,699
Scottish Courts Administration	981
Scottish Record Office	125
General Register Office (Scotland)	286
Registers of Scotland[5]	1,322
The Scottish Office and Associated Departments Total	13,413

Notes: [1] Full-time equivalents as at 31 December 1992

[2] Includes staff of the Scottish Fisheries Protection Agency (263) and Scottish Agricultural Science Agency (150)

[3] Includes staff of the agency, Historic Scotland (693)

[4] Includes staff of the Scottish Prison Service (4,577)

[5] Executive agency

Printed by HMSO, Edinburgh Press
Dd 0287622 5M 3/93 (209344)